Brookgreen

G A R D E N S

Wyrick & Company

Published by Wyrick & Company
1-A Pinckney Street
Charleston, SC 29401

Copyright © 1999 by Brookgreen Gardens

Text written by Kennedy Kipps
Book design by Paul Rossmann
Printed in Hong Kong

Library of Congress Cataloging-in-Publication Data

Photo credits: Carlton Abbott, 11(l.), 13, 28 (r.);
Charles Slate, 4, 7 (top), 34, 36; Susan Stambaugh,
front cover, 15, 19 (r.), 24, 40, 44 (l.); Virginia Weiler:
2, 5, 8, 10, 23, 27, 33, 35, 42, 44 (r.), back cover;
Reggie Williams, 32, 37; Charles Wyrick, 9, 14, 16 (r.),
17. All other photographs courtesy Brookgreen
Gardens.

> *cover:* Carl Milles,
> *The Fountain of the Muses*

> *title page:* Anna Hyatt Huntington,
> *Fighting Stallions*

> Richard McDermott Miller,
> *Wind on the Water*

BROOKGREEN GARDENS

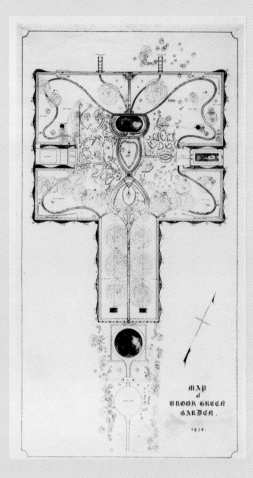

Brookgreen Gardens is a remarkable place. Its rich layering of art, garden, native animals, and wilderness has been shaped by the generations of people who have called this land home. Brookgreen has many stories to tell. Each year thousands of visitors come to hear them.

Covering 9,000 acres of the South Carolina Lowcountry stretching from the Atlantic Ocean to the Waccamaw River, Brookgreen today is best known for its beautiful display garden and superb sculpture collection. The surrounding woodland and tidal swamp display an array of native plants and animals and are the setting for tours that address the site's cultural and ecological history.

At Brookgreen's heart, both literally and figuratively, is the thirty-acre display garden, an enticing arrangement of decorative plants, representational sculpture, and tablets engraved with poetry. The combination of these three elements is key to the garden's appeal.

The core of the garden is divided into individual rooms with major sculptures anchoring their centers. Surrounding the featured works in the Palmetto Garden and Dogwood Garden, for example, are pools of water, raised planting beds, pathways, and walls that together organize the room's structure. But plants bring these garden rooms vitality.

By virtue of their color, texture, or arrangement, the trees, shrubs, and flowers provide an organic framework that defines the composition. The rows of palmetto trees that seem to be marching around the

perimeter of the Palmetto Garden evoke the Mediterranean inspiration for this room more clearly than any architectural feature. Similarly, the finely branched dogwoods of the garden room that bears their name create a lace-like accompaniment to four classic stone sculptures of reclining women.

Many times at Brookgreen, sculpture and plants interact on a truly massive scale. Monumental works of art routinely provide a distant focal point at the end of a long path or shine through an opening framed by trees. More often, however, the interplay of nature and art is a quiet, easy friendship like that exemplified by the small sculptures and colorful perennials that occupy the niches in the garden's many serpentine walls.

The strong sight lines that draw visitors along its walkways make

right: Clio Hinton Bracken, *Chloe*

Brookgreen an engaging garden to explore. Overlaid on the remnants of a nineteenth-century rice plantation, the garden design takes maximum advantage of a spectacular double file of live oaks that once led to Brookgreen Plantation's main house.

Following the live oak allée, and extending well beyond it in both directions, the garden's main axis slices through a series of garden rooms punctuated by sculpture and pools of water. The clean, driven design was conceived during the 1930s by sculptor Anna Hyatt Huntington, who founded Brookgreen Gardens with her husband, Archer Milton

Elie Nadelman, *Resting Stag*

Huntington, a gentleman-scholar and philanthropist from New York.

Anna Huntington balanced formal rectilinear garden rooms with a more naturalistic upper garden where light gray walkways trace the outline of a butterfly with outstretched wings. Remnants of boxwood hedges remain from the original plantation landscape, and now people and animals rendered in bronze and stone peek from behind them.

The garden's plants present different visual backdrops throughout the year. While azaleas and dogwood draw

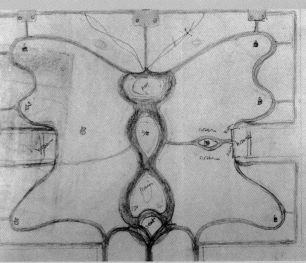

top: *Early aerial view of Brookgreen*
above: *Mrs. Huntington's garden plan, 1932*

far left: Anna Hyatt Huntington,
The Visionaries, detail

left: Anna Hyatt Huntington,
Archer Milton Huntington

attention to themselves as they flaunt the glories of spring, the bare branches that follow eight months later allow the winter light to cast the garden's sculptures in high relief.

Brookgreen also varies its plant palette according to the character of individual garden rooms. The blazing reds, oranges, and yellows of cannas, lantana, daylilies, and oleander reflect the heat of summer along the especially sun-drenched approach to Saint-Gaudens' *Diana (left)*. The pairing of arching, tufted grasses with the playful *Fountain of the Muses* makes a subtle reference to the sculpture's whimsicality. Near the entrance to the display garden, a steady succession of white flowers and plants with silver-gray foliage underscores the serenity of a still pool surrounding the graceful *Diana of the Chase*.

left: Augustus Saint-Gaudens, *Diana*
below: Carl Milles, *The Fountain of the Muses,* detail

UNPARALLELED ARTISTRY

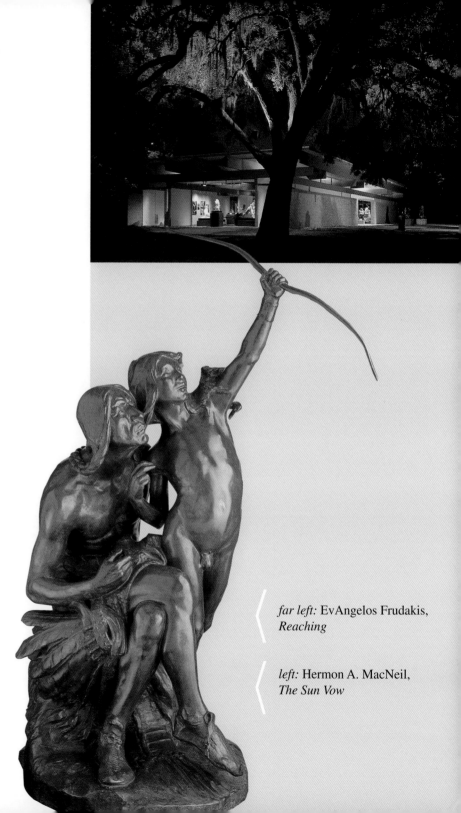

Brookgreen is justly famous for its delightful presentation of sculpture in a garden setting. It is equally well known for the quality of its sculpture collection. Quite simply, Brookgreen's collection of American representational sculpture is unrivalled by any other holding, public or private, for the number of works it contains (more than 725) and the number of artists represented (nearly 300).

Brookgreen is an institution that exhibits nearly all of its

far left: EvAngelos Frudakis, *Reaching*

left: Hermon A. MacNeil, *The Sun Vow*

holdings all of the time. Most are shown outdoors in the display garden. A number of works needing some protection from the weather are exhibited in the Mary Alice and Bennett A. Brown Sculpture Court (opposite page), and temporary thematic exhibitions are staged in the galleries of the Callie and John Rainey Sculpture Pavilion near the garden entrance.

The collection includes only sculpture by American artists from the early nineteenth century to the present, with a concentration of works in metal from 1885 to 1940. Among the artists included are such well-known figures as Daniel Chester French (below), Augustus Saint-Gaudens (left), Frederick MacMonnies, Paul Manship, and Carl Paul Jennewein.

The focus on representational works–mostly people and animals–rather than on abstract sculpture is also unusual, and gives the collection one of its signal strengths: a cohesiveness that allows the sculptures to work well with each other and in the garden setting. Brookgreen's unwavering attention

left: Augustus Saint-Gaudens, *The Puritan*

right: Daniel Chester French, *Benediction*

far right: Marshall Fredericks, *The Wings of the Morning*

12

to a single artistic tradition has created a collection with great depth, in contrast to those of institutions that have chosen to interpret the breadth of artistic trends.

The sculpture collection was begun during the 1930s, when the Huntingtons purchased Brookgreen Plantation and began to construct the public display garden. Anna's *Diana of the Chase*, Carl Paul Jennewein's *Comedy*, and Chester Beach's *Sylvan* were among the works from their private collection that the Huntingtons first gave to the fledgling garden.

In 1934, Anna placed her *Diana* in a round pool just outside the walled garden that contained the live oak allée. Two bronze lions she had originally created for the Hispanic Society of America were then stationed at the entrance to the Diana pool, carefully aligned with the live oaks in order to establish the basis of the garden's main axis–one of its strongest design elements. To extend this axis eastward, her *Youth Taming the Wild*, a monumental limestone of a young man calming a frenzied horse, was placed in a pond almost half a mile east. Edward McCartan's gilded bronze *Dionysus (right)* and Nathaniel Choate's *Alligator Bender (left)* marked the continuation of the imaginary line westward, toward the edge of the old rice fields.

The collection includes more works executed during the 1930s than any other period,

left: Nathaniel Choate, *Alligator Bender*

right: Edward McCartan, *Dionysus*

15

corresponding, in large measure, to the initial surge of construction at the garden. The Huntingtons purchased some sculptures through dealers but often bought works directly from the artists and gave them to Brookgreen. Because commissions for sculpture were scarce during the Great Depression, the Huntingtons' acquisitions were an important source of income for sculptors, particularly those who were less well known but who, in the judgment of the couple, showed great talent.

Although collecting slowed in the 1940s and '50s, the final large works commissioned by the Huntingtons for Brookgreen were acquired during this period. These include Laura Gardin Fraser's *Pegasus,* Gleb Derujinsky's *Samson and the Lion,* A.A. Weinman's *Riders of the Dawn (below, and detail right),* and Albert Wein's *Phyrne Before the Judges,* four major compositions that anchor the spaces adjoining the display garden's main axis.

above and right: A.A. Weinman, *Riders of the Dawn*

far right: A.A. Weinman, *Riders of the Dawn,* detail

In the 1970s, Brookgreen began to seek additional works, concentrating on pieces that expanded the chronological period represented in the collection. The acquisition of marbles done during the first half of the nineteenth century by artists such as Hiram Powers created a link to the earliest generation of American sculptors. The addition of works by contemporary sculptors, such as *Gazelle* by Marshall Fredericks and *Fountain of the Muses* by Carl Milles in the 1970s, and more recently, the immensely popular *Pledge Allegiance* by Glenna Goodacre (right) and the most-often-photographed sculpture in the gardens, Derek Wernher's *Len Ganeway (left)*, reflects a continuing practice that keeps the Brookgreen collection vital.

19

far left: Derek Wernher, *Len Ganeway*

below left: Paul Manship, *Evening*

below: Glenna Goodacre, *Pledge Allegiance*

SURROUNDED BY NATURE

In contrast to the orderly design and organization of the display garden, the Lowcountry landscape surrounding it seems virtually untouched by man, but only at first glance. The garden sits on Brookgreen Plantation, one of four contiguous antebellum rice plantations the Huntingtons purchased in 1930. Today the neighboring plantations, Springfield, Laurel Hill, and The Oaks, have reverted to forest and swamp. Like the Brookgreen Plantation, however, they were subjected during the eighteenth century and the early nineteenth century to one of the most systematic and extensive landscape alterations in American history. Situated on a narrow peninsula bordered on the east by the Atlantic Ocean and on the west by the Waccamaw River, they contained swampland that proved ideal for growing rice, a crop that brought handsome returns but required grueling work. Ready markets and slave labor brought extraordinary wealth to the region a century and a half ago.

The Oaks Plantation, the southernmost of the four comprised in the present landholding, is also the lowest in elevation. Its vast stretches of longleaf pine

right: C. Paul Jennewein, *Nymph and Fawn*

21

trees are typical of its sandy, and often soggy, soil. Thanks to recent archaeological investigations, the foundation of the plantation's main house is visible in a clearing near where the rice fields began. The size of the foundation, however, suggests a structure smaller than the one modern visitors might imagine for the home of Joseph Alston, a powerful planter who married the daughter of Aaron Burr, the third vice president of the United States, and who was elected South Carolina's governor in 1812.

The brick wall and raised monuments of the adjacent Alston family cemetery are an ideal habitat for several types of ferns and mosses not usually found in this area. Not far away, the longleaf pines provide similarly advantageous circumstances for several uncommon animal species.

The northern end of the Brookgreen property, by contrast, has a decidedly upland feeling. The former Laurel Hill Plantation rises and falls over geological formations called xeric sandhills–the massive sand dunes deposited here by the ocean millions of years before anyone thought of planting rice. The vegetation includes longleaf pine, scrappy looking turkey oaks, and wonderful carpets of fluffy, gray-green reindeer moss.

At The Oaks, dry land is barely above creek level, but at Laurel Hill the forest yields to a commanding view of the Waccamaw River from a 25-foot-high bluff. Laurel Hill's main house, like those of the other plantations, is only a memory; but evidence of it remains in the form of a broad live oak allée. Nearby, a 100-foot-tall, star-shaped brick chimney marks the site of the large plantation's rice mill.

Recently, small numbers of Brookgreen visitors in the company of staff interpreters have begun to see these extremes of the property, primarily through the fall EcoAdventures program with its hiking, horseback riding, biking, camping, and kayaking activities. Larger numbers of visitors can easily get a good view of the Lowcountry habitat from the John and Caroline Lumpkin Ricefield Overlook or aboard "The Springfield," Brookgreen's tour boat that follows the tidal creeks along the property's Waccamaw River edge.

left: Gleb Derujinsky, *Samson and the Lion*

right: Benjamin F. Hawkins, *Triton on Dolphin*

ALLIGATORS AND FOXES

Exhibits along the Lowcountry Trail at Brookgreen give visitors an opportunity to see, up close, many of the native animals and plants that populate the area's ecosystem.

The most extensive exhibit is the aviary in the cypress swamp section of the trail. In 1977, Brookgreen covered a half-acre of existing tidal swampland in a black fabric net. The enclosure soars above bald cypress and black gum trees, wax myrtle bushes, and other native plants. Supported by poles as tall as 90 feet anchored to concrete pilings sunk some 60 feet into the swamp, the mesh tent retains a group of large aquatic birds while allowing many swamp inhabitants to move freely in and out of the exhibit. Turtles, fish, snakes, and native songbirds easily pass through the wide-meshed netting. The cypress aviary is so large and so thoroughly integrated into the surrounding swamp, in fact, that visitors hardly notice the netting as they walk along its boardwalk.

The herons, egrets, ducks, and ibis that live in the exhibit are all native to the South Carolina Lowcountry and are natural residents of swamp or marsh habitats. But because their numbers are concentrated in the aviary, visitors are more

left: Joseph Nicolosi, *Dream*

right: Anna Hyatt Huntington, *Diana of the Chase*

likely to see them there than in the sur-rounding landscape.

Playful North American river otters are included along the tidal creek section of the Lowcountry Trail, where the water flowing through their exhibit naturally rises and falls with the changing tide. The adjacent exhibit contains a more deadly inhabitant of the tidal creek environment, the frightening but fascinating American alligator. During the period of rice cultivation, alligators often threatened the fields by digging tunnels into the dikes that defined them.

As visitors move to the upland forest portion of the trail, they see exhibits that feature red and gray foxes, white-tailed deer, and birds of prey. Both species of fox can climb the sloping trees in their exhibit and tunnel underground to keep cool or rear their young. The red and gray foxes are housed together so visitors can easily compare and contrast the behaviors of these animals that share a common Lowcountry habitat.

The trail's white-tailed deer live in a twelve-acre fenced savannah bordered by forest. Extremely shy, these animals, the largest that inhabit the Lowcountry, are rarely seen in the wild. Despite their size, deer can render themselves nearly invisible because of their markings and their ability to remain motionless. However, along the Lowcountry

left: Anna Hyatt Huntington, *Wild Boars*

right: Albert Wein, *Phryne Before the Judges*

26

Trail the chances of seeing these beautiful animals improve greatly.

The raptor aviary, a second mesh tent that visitors can walk through, holds eagles, owls, hawks, and vultures. Like many animals at the park, most of these birds are classified as "unreleasables." They would be unable to survive in the wild either because of injuries or because they are too reliant on people. Their presence at Brookgreen, therefore, is as important to their health as it is valuable to the visitors who, by seeing them, come to better understand the native creatures of the Lowcountry.

left: C. Paul Jennewein,
The Greek Dance

right: Ernest Haswell,
Little Lady of the Sea

ON THE RIVER

More than any other force, man's activity has shaped the history and ecology of the Lowcountry. Nowhere at Brookgreen is that more evident than in the vast acreage of former rice fields. From the Lumpkin Overlook, it is easy to follow the lines of trees growing on the old dikes that bounded the field immediately beneath it. Wooden trunks with swinging gates, once used to control water levels in the fields, have been restored in the dike here.

Carolina Gold rice, the historic cash crop of this region, has long since given way in the abandoned fields to other aquatic plants such as pickerel weed, yellow primrose, cattails, and a native wild rice that is an

far left: Anna Hyatt Huntington, *Youth Taming the Wild*

below: Katharine Lane Weems, *Greyhounds Unleashed*

important food source for birds. In addition to the vista from the Lumpkin Overlook, Brookgreen offers seasonal excursions on "The Springfield" for a closer look at this special habitat.

The complex story of the rice plantations and the men and women who lived and worked on them is recounted during

left, and detail below: Paul Manship, *Time and the Fates of Man*

right: Bryant Baker, *The Afternoon of the Faun*

these excursions. By 1840, Brookgreen, along with The Oaks, Springfield, and Laurel Hill, was among some forty rice plantations fronting on the Waccamaw River in Georgetown County. During those days, half the nation's rice crop was produced in the Georgetown district, and the rice plantation owners were among the nation's elite. Slavery made it possible.

The first colonial settlers in Carolina were drawn from the Caribbean, and African slaves were among them. It was the African slaves, not their European masters, who possessed the knowledge necessary to impound fields and cultivate rice. And, of course, it was also the slaves who provided the labor.

To understand the magnitude of their technical achievement, one need only compare the endless fields of rice in 1840 to the virgin swamp forest the slaves had begun to clear by the end of the seventeenth century.

Growing rice requires flat fields that can be flooded and drained at will. To create such fields, the slaves had to fell hardwood trees as large as ten feet in diameter, remove the timber, dig out the stumps, level the land, and then build the dikes, trenches, and gates that allowed them to control the water level. They did it all with simple hand tools, standing knee-deep in mud and water with the added stress of alligators and poisonous snakes, not to mention extremely high temperatures and humidity. Developing a typical rice field that covered between forty and seventy acres could take up to ten years.

The slaves' expertise came from West Africa, where the climate and methods for growing rice in the Angola and Senegambia regions were nearly identical to those of South Carolina. Planters placed orders for slaves to be

right: Charles Keck, *Fauns at Play*

35

acquired from specific regions grounded in the rice culture because their knowledge of rice cultivation was so valuable.

The process of growing and harvesting rice was equally complex. First, the dry fields were cultivated in early spring. In April, slaves dropped grains of rice into prepared trenches, covering the seeds with their feet as they went along. The fields were then flooded for several days while the rice sprouted. Next, slaves drained and hoed the fields, then flooded, drained, and hoed them again. The longest stretch of dry field cultivation ran from early June through mid July–full days of hoeing in the summer heat. A third flooding, from mid July through mid September, supported the slender rice plants with their heavy ripening seed heads. After a final draining, the slaves cut the rice stalks with sickles and prepared the grain for market.

The rice plantations of the Waccamaw used a task system in contrast to tobacco and cotton plantations where slaves worked in mass from sunrise to sunset. Each day except Sunday every rice plantation slave was assigned a task, a specific amount of work that was expected to be accomplished that day. Tasks varied according to the age, strength, and ability of the slave.

Once the task was completed, the slave could spend any remaining part of the day as he wished–perhaps in activities that supported his household or by helping another slave who was having difficulty completing his assigned task. Those who did not complete their task, who attempted to escape, or who broke other rules of the plantation master and overseers were punished, often physically and severely.

far right: Anna Hyatt Huntington, *Don Quixote*

36

CHANGING STATUS

The American Civil War brought freedom to the slaves and an end to the planters' inexpensive labor source. The War was followed by a few untimely hurricanes during harvest, and rice cultivation on the Waccamaw waned, bringing to an end the region's status as a center of wealth and power.

By the 1930s, Archer and Anna Huntington were able to buy four of the old rice plantations and begin yet another slow transformation of this land. Until they died, he in 1955 and she in 1973, they worked diligently to achieve their vision of a beautiful sculpture garden and a site for preserving the plants and animals of the area.

Today Brookgreen Gardens, the educational institution they founded in 1931, is fulfilling the Huntingtons' vision by ever more tightly interweaving the many stories this land can tell into a comprehensive interpretation of the South Carolina Lowcountry for a more detailed exploration of Brookgreen's history and ecology.

Brookgreen's heritage–cultural, natural, and artistic–is richly layered. For some people, including those Brookgreen employees who trace their lineage back a generation to the men and women hired by the Huntingtons to build the garden, and then back several more generations to the slaves who worked the same ground, the connection to that heritage is as tangible as the sculptures that now dot the property.

Perhaps less directly, that heritage also affects every visitor to Brookgreen Gardens. From the role that slavery has played in the evolution of modern American culture and the ecological impact of man's relentless reshaping of the land, to the view of humanity reflected in bronze or stone and the powerful sense of serenity that this skillfully designed display garden evokes, Brookgreen speaks on many levels. For the visitor who asks questions, who explores, and who draws connections, Brookgreen can begin a compelling dialogue.

left: Anna Hyatt Huntington, *Jaguar*

top right: Berthold Nebel, *Nereid*

bottom right: Frederic Remington, *Bronco Buster*

REVISING A GARDEN

The display garden Anna Hyatt Huntington designed for Brookgreen in the 1930s featured a lean, driven design with strong sight lines and impressive focal points. Seven decades later, the face of Brookgreen has been changed by the addition of works by a new generation of American sculptors, plantings that greatly enhance the original design, and increased visitation.

During the mid-1990s, Brookgreen decided to direct more attention to the horticultural aspects of the garden and at the same time to launch a traveling exhibition, "American Masters: Sculpture from Brookgreen Gardens." In tandem, these decisions were the impetus for reviewing some 60 years of accretive change in the garden.

With some sculptures temporarily removed for the exhibition, the strong focus of Anna Huntington's earliest garden rooms was revealed. New, simplified plantings further underscored her design restraint.

Beneath the live oak allée, for example, Brookgreen's gardeners created a contrasting understory of lush turf and undulating mulch beds. Around the garden room's perimeter, dwarf mondo grass and *Podocarpus*, an evergreen shrub, now provide quiet, yearlong interest at the foot of the serpentine wall. Color is reserved for the eye-level raised beds where sculpture and flowering

perennials are tucked into the curving niches.

The narrow concrete pathways of the 1930s in the upper garden presented a problem for modern Brookgreen: their width would accommodate neither maintenance vehicles nor the current number of visitors. Widening was inevitable, yet it had to be done in a way that maintained the fabric and feeling of Anna Huntington's original paths. The solution was to line the walks with rows of dark brown brick that blend in with the plantings. Visually, the paths still follow a narrow, light gray line.

The growth of nearby resort communities began to bring visitors to Brookgreen throughout the year, so the garden needed color well beyond the show-stopping flush of April azaleas. Now a succession of flowering trees, shrubs, and perennials in raised beds and containers offers horticultural interest all year.

In addition, upgrades of the garden's electrical and irrigation systems have enhanced maintenance and permitted installation of a distinctive illumination system used when the garden is open at night.

While visitors are increasingly lured to Brookgreen by its horticultural quality alone, it is still the distinctive combination of garden and sculpture–established well over six decades ago–that invites them to linger and to return.

left: Mario Korbel, *Sonata*

right: Anna Hyatt Huntington, *Diana of the Chase*

DEVELOPING A SITE FOR SCULPTURE

Sculpture placed in an outdoor setting provides visual delights and poses unique problems. While Brookgreen's sculpture is stationary, the settings for these works of art change–month by month as plants grow and bloom, and hour by hour as the angle of the sun shifts from dawn to dusk.

The right plant choices can emphasize the serenity of a sculpture or accentuate its lightheartedness. Some plants can dominate a setting in one season, and give way to the work of art in the next. Such plant transformations affect the way visitors view Brookgreen's sculpture, especially if it is seen in different seasons and on return visits.

The effects of changing light, on the other hand, are far more rapid. In the strong sunlight of noon, some works of art at Brookgreen may seem to be just enormous chunks of stone, but they are redefined (and, in a sense, re-created) in the golden rays of the setting sun and yet again in the soft moonlight of early evening.

One of Brookgreen's major strengths, its complex combination of plants and sculpture, may also be its biggest challenge. The sheer number of things to see can lead to sensory overload, especially for first-time visitors. Brookgreen's curators recommend coming back at different times of day and during different seasons to fully appreciate the artistry of the sculpture in its changing garden setting.

Compatibility is the true measure of success in the placement of outdoor sculpture. A work of art and its plant setting should give a viewer the

above: Hope Yandell,
Lioness and Cub

far left: Paul Fjelde,
Nymph

43

feeling that they were virtually made for each other, as indeed do the combinations of sculpture and landscape design at Brookgreen. Paul Manship's *Diana*, at the boundary of the display garden, seems about to spring to life as a true goddess of the hunt and leap through the nearby abandoned rice fields. The shyness of *My Niece* by Joe Davidson is accentuated by the delicate screen of Siberian irises she seems to be hiding behind. And where else could Edith Parson's *Frog Baby* be except exuberantly splashing away in the pool in the new Garden Room for Children?

These pairings, like dozens more throughout Brookgreen, meet one of the collection's major goals: when a visitor sees a sculpture in its outdoor setting, the combination should feel absolutely right.

PRESERVING NATURE'S RARITIES

Surrounding the carefully designed display garden and its adjacent Lowcountry Trail, a vast tract of wilderness is managed by Brookgreen as a natural history conservation zone.

The Brookgreen property is filled with plants and animals common to its swamp and forest habitats, from cypress trees and reindeer moss to alligators and wild turkeys. But because of careful forest management and an occasional quirk of circumstance, the land is also home to many kinds of wildlife found in few other places.

Brookgreen's most uncommon resident is the endangered red-cockaded woodpecker. This small bird, similar in size to the more familiar downy woodpecker, requires a specific habitat: a stand of tall longleaf pines with little undergrowth. Furthermore, some of the trees have to be afflicted by red heart disease so the woodpeckers can carve out their distinctive nesting cavities.

In partnership with governmental agencies and private environmental organizations, Brookgreen regularly cuts undergrowth and undertakes controlled burns in its longleaf pine forest to provide a clear area for these small woodpeckers to forage. The birds have

above: Anna Hyatt Huntington, *Fighting Stallions*

far left: Paul Manship, *Diana*

below: James Earle Fraser, *The End of the Trail*

responded by nesting and raising their young in slowly increasing numbers. Brookgreen's managed forest is also home to a number of bald eagles, now classified as a threatened species.

Beneath the forest floor, certain small burrows dug in the sandy soil reveal the presence of the gopher tortoises that also benefit from Brookgreen's forest management. This species is rarely found beyond such protected locations because of the diminishing woodland areas and the infrequency of forest fires that are followed by the natural replenishment of its preferred undergrowth-free habitat.

The unusual environment in the Alston family cemetery, albeit man-made, has become an ideal setting for several species of Lowcountry plants that flourish in unique habitats. The bricks and mortar used to build the cemetery walls provide minerals and water-retaining crevices that nourish quite a few of these plants, including varieties of moss, spleenwort, liverwort, and–in a touch of natural irony–resurrection fern.

Brookgreen's Lowcountry Trail also serves the institution's conservation goals by helping to provide a home for individual native animals that could not survive on their own. And because some species in the collection, such as the cypress aviary's black-crowned night herons, reproduce so prolifically, Brookgreen can share Lowcountry natives with zoos elsewhere.